# TWO TIME
# HALL OF FAME

## BY WAYNE BOOKER

WB
PUBLISHING

Published in the United States of America
ISBN: 978-0-578-11010-3

WWW.WAYNEBOOKER.COM

# This book is dedicated to . . .

my mother, the late Bobbie Jean Bland-Booker, my father, Ned Andrew Booker Sr., and all my family members.

all of my coaches, teachers, and friends because if you hadn't believed in me or pushed me, I would not have written this book.

my wife, Gwendolyn Bufford-Booker. Thanks for encouraging me to write this book.

# INTRODUCTION

In September 2008, Kenneth Dewayne [Wayne] Booker received an unexpected telephone call that changed his life for the better. It was a call that every athlete hopes to receive, but doesn't dare dream of actually getting. It is because of that telephone call that he decided to tell his story. It is that same telephone call that proved to him the Bible to be true in stating that your gift will make room for you. What is this gift? Wayne's gift is shown in his everyday walk in servanthood to others........

# ACKNOWLEDGMENTS

I have finally finished my first book. I want to thank, first and foremost, my LORD and SAVIOUR, JESUS CHRIST. None of this would be possible without Him.

There are so many people, whose names I'd like to call, but I will only mention a few.

I would like to thank Tracee L. Taylor for recommending Jackie Welch to me after my searching so diligently for someone to assist me. Jackie Welch, I don't know what I would have done without you.

Thanks to Leroy Watson, Jr. for helping me out with the questions and knowledge on how to write this book.

Sidney Shields, it seems that we were all over Memphis taking pictures for this project; thanks, man.

Robert Powell, the layout is great.

Thanks to Carlee McCullough, my attorney, for making sure that all legal issues were in order.

Four years ago I told cheri wells, my editor, that I wanted to tell this story. She said, "If you write it, I'll edit it." Thanks Ms. wells.

To my church family, keep praying for me!

To my older daughter, Chelsea Newble, remember that it was at a basketball game that someone discovered you, and now you have become a model for catalogues and magazines. You never know who's watching you. Continue to work hard, maintain your honor status in the classroom, and work to be the best in modeling.

To my younger daughter, Mallori Lois Booker, who plays basketball in Marietta, Georgia. I want you to see that it takes hard work and that you have to put in the work to get better. Whatever you put in is what is going to come out. So work hard all the time both on the court and in the classroom. Keep those grades up.

In memory of my mother, Bobbie Jean Booker . . . thanks for being there for me all the time.

# CHAPTER 1

Wayne grew up in Memphis, Tennessee with a childhood that was no different from many kids during his time. He was raised by both of his parents in a home where praying and being obedient to your parents were part of everyday life. He was the fourth son and followed in the footsteps of his older brothers by participating in a variety of sports. Wayne tried his hand at them all, but he had a passion for basketball and was very skilled at it. Throughout elementary school every kid had ambition, except Wayne; there was none for him.

Wayne's parents always encouraged him to get an education. Ned and Bobbie Jean Booker were lifelong productive citizens of Coffeeville, Mississippi, in Yalobusha County. During their lifetime, they had learned the importance of their children getting a good education. Wayne was the fifth of six children (one sister and four brothers): Narvel Louise, Robert, Ned Jr., Larry, and Ronald. His parents weren't strict, but they stressed three things: get an education, respect elders, and perform chores - you had to put in the work. All the boys had to work at their Uncle Joe's barber shop (Bland's Barber Shop), shining shoes. They worked every day after school and all day on Saturdays.

Wayne experienced his parents' hard work ethic one summer while visiting both sets of grandparents, Earline Bland and Alfred *Alf* and Mary Booker. He and his brothers, along with their cousin, Kim McManis, learned firsthand about their grandparents' work in the fields of Mississippi. They started work at 4:30 in the morning, so they could work before it got too hot. The work included hauling watermelons, gardening, etc. Wayne would use the hoe to chop dirt, but he didn't like the early rising and hard manual work. His grandmother let him know that without an education he, too, would do this every day. Wayne decided right then that he would not be doing that for a living. His grandparents showed their grandchildren at an early age the importance of getting an education, and his parents kept reiterating that fact.

While attending Shannon Elementary in the Hyde Park district of north Memphis, his teachers would tell him to take school and his studies seriously because playing ball would not last. Wayne played ball with his older brothers and other friends. They helped him to develop his skills. His older brothers, Robert, Ned Jr. and Larry, would whip him at every opportunity so he, in turn, would whip his younger brother, Ronald. All of his brothers were athletes.

Wayne attempted to play football on a community team, but he wasn't really interested in football. He was trying to follow in his brothers' footsteps. His ex-brother-in-law gave him a video camera to record one of the football games. He knew from recording the game that football wasn't for him. He tried out for football at Cypress Junior High School, went to practice with his brother, Larry, but the practice was cancelled that day. Wayne never went back. He also tried his hand at baseball. He couldn't hit the ball. He played pitcher and outfielder. No, baseball was not for him either.

Wayne decided to start The Olympic Games within the neighborhood. He made his own medals; 1st, 2nd and 3rd places earned medals. The Games consisted of baseball, shot put, long jump, swimming meets, and relay races. It was an adventurous summer for everyone. The competitors included Donald Green, Jerald *J-Bird* Starks, the late Cassell Harris, William *Apple Jack* Phillips Jr., the late Dan *Danny Boy* Green, and Wayne's brothers. They had all the field events, all the sprint events, and used a baseball for the shot put. Wayne created the Olympics to determine who the best athlete was. The field called, *The Levy* was used for the long jump. Gooch Swimming Pool held all swim categories. Everyone was good at something, which made the competition so good and each event so exciting. That is when his competitiveness started.

While he was attending Shannon Elementary, Wayne started hanging out with his older friends. He tried drinking and marijuana at an early age and found it easy to get caught up with friends and hard to say no. He was shooting dice and pitching pennies and quarters while at school. But he soon discovered that there was no growth in that circle. Kids may stray from what their parents have taught them. It isn't that parents don't know what kids are doing, but parents allow kids to make their own choices. They choose to be obedient or they choose to be disobedient. It's not always a reflection on the parents.

Wayne had two sets of friends. He had the friends who chose to do what was right. He also had the friends who chose to do what was wrong. He once took money that didn't belong to him. When Larry Bland, Sr. discovered that Wayne had taken the money, he and Uncle Joe sent him home. Although Wayne was sixteen at the time, his father gave him the worse whipping he'd ever had. He understood that there were consequences for his actions. He never took any money that wasn't his again. He found that he was getting caught in the wrong circle and that playing sports was his way out.

Wayne's mother's family (Pete and Mary Bland) had a family reunion every year. His immediate family always attended. During the reunion, every family had to announce accomplishments. It didn't register to Wayne until later in life how important the reunions were and what announcing each family's accomplishments meant. Reality set in and he realized that being recognized for an accomplishment was to be taken seriously. His maternal side of the family - the Blands - believed in four things: GOD, family, education, and helping others. These four things were mentioned during every family reunion. Every reunion consisted of a Friday night meet-and-greet session. A banquet was held on Saturday, during which time the accomplishments and accolades were announced. Sunday was the time for giving help to the family wherever it was needed. It was a great learning experience for young Booker.

Wayne grew up in the church. He knew the importance of helping others from his time at Macedonia Baptist Church in Hyde Park. His parents made sure their children always participated in some form of service at church. It wasn't until his sophomore year of high school that Wayne began hanging with the right crowd. He discovered that the group he hung with included positive people doing something positive with their lives, and he wanted to be a part of that circle.

# CHAPTER 2

After leaving Shannon Elementary School, Wayne was enrolled in Cypress Junior High School. He was used to playing community center basketball, so he decided to try out for the basketball team at school. He not only made the team in the seventh grade, but under the direction of Coach Odell Harris, he was also a starter. He made the team again in the eighth grade, this time under Coach Brogan, and was a starter once more.

Wayne had gotten comfortable with his basketball success, so imagine the shock and dismay he felt when he tried out for the team in the ninth grade and was cut! He was hurt and decided to throw in the towel. He decided he would give up on school ball and just continue playing community ball for Coach Joseph Norman, Sr. and Coach Phillips at the YMCA. He could once again feel confident in his basketball abilities.

The next year ~~Booker~~ Wayne attended Douglass High School. Wayne had the idea that it was a different school and a different atmosphere - different. He felt because he had continued to improve on his basketball skills through the community center that he would surely make the school's basketball team. Once again he was cut! The other team players and his friends knew how well he played and what an asset Wayne would be to the team, so they got together and asked the coach why Wayne was cut from the team. The coach wasn't really sure who Wayne was and asked him to try out again. But pride had stepped in and Wayne refused to try out. He decided to go where he knew he was comfortable and felt appreciated. He went back to playing for Coach Norman. At the end of his tenth-grade year, he left Douglass High School and was bussed to Kingsbury High School.

As Wayne began that school year at Kingsbury High School, he was optimistic. It was a fresh new school with a fresh new start and fresh new possibilities. His friends tried to persuade him to try out for basketball. He was so frustrated about his 9th- and 10th-grade years of being cut that he once again refused to try out. He decided to play it safe and continue playing for Coach Norman.

Some of the guys from the school team played against Wayne, and he beat them most of the time. That added to his frustration of why he didn't make the team. It made him question himself - why not him? He made an important decision. He would not stay down and discouraged. He went to the gym and worked even harder. He was determined to prove the coaches wrong.

One of the reasons for this book is to encourage kids -male and female. Different coaches have different methods. One of the best ways to prove yourself is to work hard at whatever you choose to achieve.

Kingsbury's Coach Charles Nute went to Wayne's physical education class to ask him to try out for the basketball team. And at the end of his junior year Wayne's friends talked him into trying out for the summer league. He tried out and made the team. He was selected for the second string. One of the coach's rules was that the players must make practice unless they were sick. One of his teammates couldn't make practice because of transportation problems, and this gave Wayne the opportunity he needed to play first string during the summer league and to start the rest of the season.

# CHAPTER 3

Wayne was so glad about making first string in the summer league that he decided to put his past behind him and try out for the school team his senior year. He tried out, made it, and started on the varsity team! He played the whole season and played well. At the end of the season there was an athletic banquet. At the banquet, much to his surprise, Wayne was awarded the most improved player award. He also discovered that several coaches had been watching him. *Message: You should always put your best foot forward in attitude and work because you never know who's watching you.* Wayne still adopts that theory today.

The coach from Itawamba Community College asked if he would like to tour the school, which was located in Fulton, Mississippi, near Tupelo. Wayne was ecstatic and shouted, "Yes!" Kingsbury High School Coach Nute took Wayne and Wiley Jefferson on a tour of the college. After touring the school, Coach Nute asked Wayne if he liked the school. The reason he asked was that Coach knew it was not his job to pick the school for the student/athlete. If for some reason he didn't like the school, Wayne would know it was his choice and no one else's. He could blame no one for his decision but himself. *Wayne still adopts that theory today.*

Although Wayne knew he liked it, he visited between five and seven other schools before choosing Itawamba. Once Wayne decided, Coach Wayne Newsome came to Memphis from Itawamba to meet with Wayne's parents and to sign him. At graduation, Wayne could hardly contain himself at the sound of his name being called to attend Itawamba Junior College on a full athletic scholarship. This was a dream fulfilled for the young man, who had no ambition as a kid. This was a dream fulfilled from the young man, who was discouraged and threw in the towel several times before achieving his potential. This young man was on his way.

# CHAPTER 4

As summer quickly approached, Wayne was looking forward to his freshman year at Itawamba. He decided he needed to come in physically and mentally fit (Coach Newsome told Wayne that he had no idea what to expect of college life.). The coach made him ready by telling him how to prepare.

When the season opened, Wayne was ready to play. All went well for him during his freshman year. He learned he had to keep good grades in order to keep his scholarship. Every semester required a good GPA to keep his full-time student status. The end of the year meant another athletic banquet, at which he was given the Most Valuable Player [MVP] award. Because this award was voted on by his team members, it was truly a great honor.

Coach Newsome discovered Wayne had run track in high school, so to keep him in shape during the off season, Wayne was made a member of the track team. He competed in the one-mile relay, hurdles [rated 5th in the state], and the high jump. He finished his freshman year feeling pretty good about himself and his decision to choose Itawamba.

When his sophomore year came around, he was already physically fit. He hit the books and did conditioning year round to be ready for the season's start. He continued to keep up his grades and full-time hours to qualify as a sophomore in order to keep his scholarship. He had a goal for his sophomore year.

At the end of the year came another athletic banquet. He was once again voted MVP! He also received an honorable mention All-American. The State of Mississippi held an All-Star North vs. South Game to which he was selected. After he was selected for the All-Star team, his goal was to play very hard, rebound, and play defense. After the All-Star game he was selected as the MVP.

Scouts were watching. *You never know who is watching you.* After witnessing Wayne play, several coaches asked him to visit their schools. Because this was a junior college, he could only play two years and go on to a four-year college. He chose Southeastern Louisiana University [SLU] with Coach Ken Fortenberry. Wayne flew to Louisiana to visit. He really liked Southeastern; it was an easy decision for him to make. Wayne visited five other colleges, but he had already made up his mind. The fact that Coach Newsome from Itawamba had played for Southeastern during the 60's was an added bonus. He also appreciated that Southeastern wasn't far from his hometown.

Wayne and his friend, Tim Bowers, were roommates at SLU. During his junior year in college, Wayne was introduced to his first video game, Ms. PAC-MAN. Because of this, he was not giving full attention to his studies. He saw many other students doing what he was doing - not taking care of business. He put so many quarters into the video game, only to see if he could get the highest score. Finally, Wayne became refocused and got his studies back on track. *Message: You've got to stay focused at all times.*

Wayne's first game at SLU was played against Tennessee State University. He was fouled at the end of the game and got a two-shot foul attempt with no time left on the clock and a tie game. He hit both free throws to win the game 60-58.

# CHAPTER 5

Wayne and Tim spent the entire summer conditioning. To stay in shape they played basketball, did push-ups, and ran every day. Wayne knew that it was important to stay physically fit at all times - during the season and off season. He also knew that he had to continue to study. He listened to his parents and coaches when they told him that basketball wouldn't last forever and that he would need something to fall back on. He thanked GOD for a praying family and praying coaches. His park commission coaches, high school coaches and college coaches believed in praying both before and after every game. While at Southeastern, Wayne remembered his Christian upbringing at Macedonia Church and would thank GOD every day for everything. Both Wayne and Tim shared the same family-oriented background. They were able to connect both on and off the court.

Wayne had another successful run during his junior year. He started every game and received a lot of attention. At the end-of-season athletic banquet, Wayne's team members voted him MVP. For three years in a row, he had earned the respect of his team members voting him with the honor. What was he doing that made his fellow players think so highly of him? Was it because he did not hog the ball? Was it because he practiced so hard? Was it because he was considered a gentleman on the court as well as off? Or was it because of his daily prayer life? Whatever the reason, Wayne was definitely on the right road.

# CHAPTER 6

Before his senior year Wayne once again spent the summer conditioning. It was at this point that he actually thought about getting drafted into the NBA. He had finally found his ambition (Or it had found him.). He said that he would have another successful year of basketball. It was his final year, and he had managed to keep his grades up. He was actually dreaming of going to the NBA. His focus was no longer on studying books. He admits he should have been thinking books first, and then ball, but he was really excited about a possible career in the NBA.

There were scouts watching him at every game. He was featured in a newspaper article while at SLU, where he was called *the cool cunning prophet*. The article spoke highly of his stats, as well as his unselfishness on the court. Wayne said in the article that he wanted to sign with a school where he would have a chance to play. It went on to say that Itawamba Coach Newsome had recommended Southeastern. Wayne still says that if he had to do it all over again he would choose SLU.

When he was signed, Wayne flatly told Coach Fortenberry that he would give him two winning seasons. After leading a win over Nicholls State, which clinched the SLU Lions a second straight winning season with their 14th victory of the year, Wayne gave his coach a wink and said, "I told you so." "It's rare for a player of Wayne Booker's ability to come through your program. From a recruiting standpoint, we feel like it will take two real good players to replace him," said Fortenberry. Needless to say, Wayne was voted co-MVP with team-mate Jerry Kelly at that year's athletic banquet. Being voted MVP all four years of college was mind blowing for Wayne. He was again invited to play in the All-Star Game. While there, he met Press Mara-vich, who suggested that Wayne's draft chances were high [Peter *Press* Maravich had been a coach at Louisiana State University, and his son was Pistol Pete Maravich.]. Press talked to Coach Fortenberry and to his parents about Wayne's chances. He also told them that Wayne needed an agent; Wayne signed with him.

# CHAPTER 7

Wayne returned home to Memphis to watch the 15-round draft at his parent's house. He listened anxiously, but at the end of the draft, his name was not called. Later that night he cried; it was the end of his dream. He was thinking of what he should do. He didn't have his degree yet, and there was no more basketball [This was in 1982, and basketball players weren't getting paid like they are now.]. His coaches and teachers advised him to complete his education. They reminded him that he had to have something to fall back on.

As he got ready for bed, his mother suggested that obviously GOD had something else planned for him; Wayne agreed. In his prayers he said that he just wanted a chance and went to bed. The next day Press Maravich called with the news that he had been offered a free agent position with the Atlanta Hawks for the summer. His prayer had been answered. So it was back to conditioning.

He went to Los Angeles to play for the Atlanta Hawks in the NBA Summer League and once there felt okay. His roommate was a guy named Mike. One very important thing he learned that summer was that the NBA was a business and that the best players not always played in the NBA. Neither he nor his roommate made it, but they both agreed to make the best out of it.

When Wayne returned home, Coach Fortenberry convinced him to return to school. He could take classes, knock them out, and get his degree. He received an offer during the last week of school from Brazil in South America to play international basketball. He was given one day to decide. He talked to his family and coaches, who told him to finish school and not take the offer. There was only a week or two left in school. His coaches encouraged him to bust his butt academically. He graduated in December of 1985 with a BA Degree in Social Welfare.

# CHAPTER 8

It is so fitting that Wayne got his degree in social welfare. His selfless attitude is genuinely displayed in his everyday walk from before college days to the present. He now spends his time working with high school kids, trying to encourage them to make the best out of life because of his wonderful experiences. He never dreamed of going to college; however, because it happened for him, he believes it can happen for any child -male or female - who has the ambition and is willing to do the work. He delivers this message: *if you do what's right, the right thing will follow you.* He reminds them that they never know who is watching to see if they are doing the right thing.

Wayne has met many coaches through other coaches because he tries hard to get kids into college. He entices them by letting them know they can meet all kinds of people through playing basketball. He has met many celebrities himself from all over the world through playing sports. But he also emphasizes the hard work that goes along with achieving success. Although he admits that college may not be for everybody, he recommends that everyone gives it a try or at least attend a trade school. Wayne's family knew the importance of education. He found out for himself that education really is the key, that there must be something to fall back on.

He still thanks GOD that he suffered no serious injuries during his basketball-playing days, but he recognizes that they do happen from time to time. He even suggests that kids should work to better themselves for the future. Time passes quickly. What you can do today, do it because you cannot go back and get that time back. Although he never dreamed of going to college, once given the opportunity, he quickly took advantage of it.

# CHAPTER 9

Since Wayne spends so much of his time helping high school students, he has made it his duty to observe their habits and attitudes. One point he has noticed is that most kids are not prepared for the incoming season. They aren't prepared for the fundamentals or the conditioning. He tries to emphasize that those two elements are key to having a successful season. Wayne takes out time to let them know that they lack the mental attitude for playing the game. He stresses that they should prepare mentally before each game and that they should prepare mentally before practice. He isn't trying to take the fun out of the game, but he knows that the right attitude and good preparation will take them far.

Another thing that Wayne stresses is that, not only do people in the stands watch them, but so do scouts. Since the coach's job is on the line, and scholarships are worth thousands of dollars, the stakes are high. Each athlete must take advantage of every opportunity.

Players also must understand that coaches ask about a player's history. Some players think they can hide their history by jumping from school to school. A coach only needs to make a phone call to find out all there is to know about a player, which is rightfully so because coaches and schools have a lot invested in the athletes through scholarships. Part of a coach's job is to call an athlete's previous school and talk to their former coaches.

They call parents, teachers, and others to find out about their investment. All coaches want respectable players. The player's attitude and his actions speak volumes. Each player leaves a record wherever he goes. Wayne lets kids know how good it is to leave a good record.

# CHAPTER 10

Entrance into the freshman year of college life, Booker says, can be tricky. He acknowledges that at first, just about everyone on the team is good. Coming from high school, the playing time may not be the same, so it is important that the player stays focused. Each player on the team could have been the star player for his school, but now everyone is on a level playing field. If everyone is a star then what would make one player stand out from the other? It's focus and commitment to everyday greatness. It's giving a consistent one hundred and ten percent at every practice and at every game. It's support from family and friends.

It is important for all players - male and female - to understand how to fit into the coach's system because each player the coach picked is good. Once a player fits, hopefully he or she will pick up the fundamentals from the high school to the college level. The player has to pick up the fundamentals of playing time as well as academics because that is where many problems begin for some athletes. This is why many athletes get into trouble on campus. Many times players transfer because of the difficulty in adjusting from one level to the next.

Players must work on fundamentals for playing every day at practice and after practice in their spare time. The entire time spent in college must consist of constantly working on the game. Why? Because someone else is always working to take your spot. Competition shows up every day. This explains why so many schools have a different line up each week. Sometimes it is because of injury, but more often than not, it is because of lack of focus. This is not only in basketball; it's in all sports. Players must be willing to look at practice game films and learn how coaches want them to play.

# CHAPTER 11

Traveling for away games is much different in college than it is in high school. Generally, the bus leaves from the school and travels that day and returns to the school the same day. The bus gets back that night or early the following morning. Wayne only spent the night in a hotel once during his junior college career, which was during the regional games.

After the games, whether at home or away, the coaches would check to see if players would do what was expected of them: after returning from an away game, the player was to get up, eat breakfast, go to class and then practice; sometimes it was practice and then class. Coaches expect their players to go to class and will check to see if they do. Following the rules and doing what is expected would determine who wanted to go to the next level. The main question asked of players is this, "Who wants to go to the next level?" The coaches would try to get a feel for the players by knowing their positive and negative characteristics. Unfortunately, some players today are not preparing themselves for the next level.

All players need to know that the recruiting coach will ask the high school coach the good, the bad and the ugly about the potential athlete. The recruiting coach tries to find out what the athlete will and won't do and his strengths and weaknesses on and off the court. Some examples of off-the-court weaknesses are skipping class, disrespect, and attitude problems.

Before recruiting a player to a junior college, coaches do a background check on the athlete's character starting as far back as middle school and on through AAU coaches. College recruiting coaches are serious about their investment and know that other coaches will be honest with them. Once an athlete is chosen and has a position on the team, he is under constant watch by the coaches. At the end of the two-year term, the coaches will determine at what school the athlete needs to continue his career/education. Some may continue on to a Division I, II, III (NCAA) or NAIA school. The process then starts over, and it gets tougher at each level because even more is being demanded of the athlete.

# CHAPTER 12

Division I is a top-notch program. A sure sign of knowing that it is top notch is travel - sometimes flying instead of riding the bus. Also, players *must* go to class. Student athletes are given an itinerary, and all classes have a syllabus. It's part of the growing process. Most kids have trouble adjusting, especially to the discipline. *Discipline is defined as doing what you're supposed to do and being where you're supposed to be both on and off the court without being told.* This is serious. Failure to do so can mean getting suspended for violating team rules. Although the coaches (head, assistant and graduate assistant) will work with the individual, the athlete, ultimately, is held accountable for being where they're supposed to be and when they're supposed to be there.

Occasionally Division I players will ride the bus to get to a game. Attitudes are always being checked, whether on the bus or on the plane. Coaches don't have time for babysitting. They are looking for well-mannered, well-behaved players. It's best to remember that no one wants to be embarrassed - not the school, your family or you, so behave accordingly.

Players should always take advantage of every positive opportunity because scholarships are based on a yearly term. At the end of the term, the coach will make an evaluation to determine if the player returns or is released. That decision is a critical one.

Division I, II, III, NAIA, and junior colleges have film sessions for the team and individuals before and after playing a game. A player can watch for his mistakes and try not to make them again. The player can see his weakness and work toward strengthening his game. The player, who puts in time watching the film, can watch himself and see his opponent's strengths and weaknesses. He can then learn from them and become a more dominant and successful player.

Freshman, Itawamba Junior College (top left)
Graduate, 1978 Kingsbury High School (top right)
SLU team, junior year (bottom)

(l-r) SLU Ass't Coach Don Wilson, Wayne Booker, Head Coach Ken Fortenberry

1977 Kingsbury High School junior year (inset)

# Booker Signs Grant
# With SE Louisiana

FULTON — Wayne Booker, twice an all-state forward at Itawamba Junior College, has accepted a scholarship at Southeastern Louisiana at Hammond, La., Coach Wayne Newsom said here Monday.

During his sophomore season Booker averaged 18.3 points per game, nine rebounds and 6.2 assists.

He is a 6-5½, 200-pound forward, who was all-state two years, most valuable player here two years and most valuable in the all-star game.

Booker was named to the all-region seven team and was an honorable mention all-American.

IJC went to the state tournament both years he played on the squad.

Earlier, Herman Bell signed at Montavalo College.

Wayne Booker

Wayne Booker and other inductees into SLU Hall of Fame

# Three Receive Scholarships

Three Memphians have signed national scholarships to play basketball in Louisiana and Texas.

Kenneth DeWayne Booker and Tim Bowers, both former Kingsbury prep stars, have signed with Southeastern Louisiana, while Robert Kirby of Whitehaven will play at Pan American.

Booker has been a standout performer at Itawamba (Miss.) Junior College for the last two campaigns under coach Wayne Newsome.

The 6-6 forward averaged 17.1 points, 9.4 rebounds and 6.1 assists per game last season with high games of 34 points and 12 rebounds.

Booker earned all-state honors two years at Itawamba and was all-regional this season, while receiving honorable mention All-America.

The most valuable player in the Mississippi Junior College all-star game, Booker was cocaptain of his team this season and has been MVP at Itawamba for two years.

Bowers, played just one year in the juco ranks, averaging seven points and two assists per game at Shelby State.

An outstanding prep performer at Kingsbury, Bowers averaged 25 points and four assists per game in his senior prep season. He earned honorable mention All-America, first team All-Memphis as well as picking up all-state, all-Metro, all district and all-regional honors.

Bowers, a 6-2 guard, broke Mike Butler's scoring record at Kingsbury during his senior season.

"We're extremely pleased to be getting these two players to join our program," said coach Ken Fortenberry. "We are getting a rebounding forward who can also score and pass along with an excellent playmaker who has shown his ability to score.

"Booker is probably the most well-rounded big man we've recruited at SLU mainly because he can do so many things so well. Because he has only played three years of organized basketball, we feel most of his game is ahead of him. The character and background of these two young men are what we are looking for in our program."

Kirby played two years at Three Rivers (Mo.) and was the "sixth man" on a Raider team which won the National Junior College Athletic Association championship two years ago with a 37-3 record.

Last season, the 6-6 Kirby started and averaged 9.8 points per game and 6.1 rebounds as Three Rivers finished at 36-5 and fifth in the nation.

"Kirby is a great prospect," said Pan American coach Jim McKone.

Newspaper article of Wayne receiving scholarships

Itawamba College
team, sophomore year
(top)

Itawamba College
team, freshman year
(middle)

SLU classmates, Jannie
Thomas Rogers and
Sharon Eubanks at
SLU induction
(bottom)

Wayne and wife, Gwen

with daughter, Mallori Lois Booker (top)
with family and friends at SLU induction (bottom)

Alfred and Mary Booker,
grandparents (top)

Earline Bland, grandmother (right)

with family and friends at the
Itawamba induction

with Keith Norman, pastor, First Baptist Church-Broad (top)
with youth of First Baptist Church-Broad (bottom)

Ned, Sr. and Bobbie Jean Booker, parents (top left)
with daughter, Chelsea Newble (top right) 3 on 3 Champions in Memphis
- Shelton Thomas, Kelvin Henderson and Wayne (bottom).

1976, siblings – (counterclockwise Wayne - lower left corner,
Ned Jr., Robert, Narvel Louise, Ronald, and Larry.)
2002, siblings and father (bottom)

Wayne and Larry Bland, Sr.
at Bland's Barber Shop on Chelsea Avenue

with Melvin Lee, pastor,
Macedonia Baptist Church
Hyde Park (above)

speaking at Itawamba Hall of Fame induction (top right)
with Kingsbury Coach Chic Nute (bottom left)
with Joey Cox, fellow Itawamba Hall of Fame inductee
(bottom right)

with SLU SID Larry Hymel, Coach Chic Nute,
SLU Grad Ass't Coach Larry Woolfolk

SLU team, senior year

1978 Kingsbury High School team

with Ned Sr. and Bobbie Jean Booker,
parents (middle)
Bobbie Jean Booker (mother) singing
"Brighter Day Ahead" (bottom right)
with daughter, Mallori Lois Booker
(bottom left)

with Nyrone Hawkins and youth they took to
St Louis Rams football game (top)
Aunts and uncles who started annual Bland family reunion (bottom)

# EPILOGUE

I wrote this book because I've always heard preachers and my pastor say, "Tell your story," so I decided to tell mine and maybe help kids in sports. I wanted to encourage them not to throw in the towel, and when given a chance, do something with the chance and make the best of the situation. I want kids to value education first and sports second. I realize that college is not for everyone [I never even thought about going.], but since I had the chance to play basketball, I did. But I decided to do basketball first and school second. I want them just to try college or get a trade and see what can come out of the situation. I want kids to try to make a better life for themselves and to become productive citizens. Whether you become a two-time Hall of Famer or not, the ultimate goal is to be the very best player you can be.

# QUOTES FROM HALL OF FAMER FANS

### Odell Harris
*7th-grade coach, Cypress Jr. High School*
Wayne's induction is a tremendous accomplishment! It all started in the 7th grade, but then he exploded in high school. Wayne had great support from his parents. They attended all of his games. He was short, but then he grew. Wayne was a memorable kid. You always remember the good and the bad; he was a good one.

### Kay Winter
*Physical education teacher, Kingsbury High School*
He was one of my favorite students. Wayne was a good student - courteous, mannerable, and disciplined, one for whom I had great admiration. His Hall of Fame inductions couldn't have happened to a nicer person. He is very deserving. He is a loving family man. He and his wife are good parents, good friends and very giving. He is a very helpful person. We need more Wayne Bookers in the world.

### Charles Chic Nute
*Coach, Kingsbury High School*
Wayne was bashful and had a bad experience getting cut from the team. His team players talked him into playing in the summer league. He made captain and was one of my leaders. He was a "no sir, yes sir" type individual. He was never arrogant and was very mannerable.

At first he had little confidence in himself, which made him easy to coach. He was a gentleman. He made all-district and all-regional and was a great rebounder, scorer and handled the ball well for his size; he was the ultimate team player. He also got along well off the court. I traveled to Itawamba and Southeastern with him. He still keeps in touch. He is well respected, unselfish, and has carried himself that way throughout life. He never let success go to his head. He is a good Christian. He was humble at his induction. I enjoyed coaching him and knowing him as a person. He didn't forget where he came from and is faithful to his schools. He did what was asked of him and is still one of my favorites.

## John Harper
*Kingsbury teammate, former NFL player*

We grew up together at Shannon Elementary School. Wayne is competitive and comes from an athletic family. He was mild and meek like Clark Kent, yet an explosive player. He has a good family background (a diamond for a mother), which passed on to the kids. He would give you the shirt off his back. We competed at Cypress Junior High and on to Kingsbury. Wayne could handle the ball, pass, and shoot like Magic Johnson - whatever coach asked of him. He was a positive role model to our classmates. He went to Itawamba College and came back doing Dr. J. I went to Southern Illinois in Carbondale. Wayne would cut out news clippings of my games and send them to me. He was a special guy. He dominated summer leagues.

He was unstoppable. What I think of his Hall of Fame awards is that they are the reflection of the person. He received his just rewards. Wayne was timely, dependable, respectful, and loving. There wasn't a mean streak in his body. He was dedicated and persistent athletically, as well as academically. He is a great example for kids today. Wayne worked at what he became. He went the extra yards. He was rejected, but he didn't give up. His talent and reflection couldn't be refused. He was committed. Transitioning from sports to regular life is not easy. You have to have something rooted in you and Wayne made the transition smoothly. He was prepared for life after sports. I consider Wayne a good dependable friend; a good family man.

**Wayne Newsome**
*Coach, Itawamba Community College*
Wayne was an excellent player and a good person, who did everything he was supposed to do. He helped keep others in line and wouldn't allow guys to break rules. He was an all-state and honorable mention All-American player. Wayne is one that comes along once in a lifetime. He calls regularly, and still attends homecoming. He is an outstanding young man. He's a cut above the rest. I can't find anything negative to say about him. He helps kids and sends them to Itawamba and other colleges. I think he should have gotten into coaching. Wayne enjoys working with young kids and is a positive influence. He keeps up with everyone from the past. Wayne is a dependable and good solid citizen. The instructors and staff at Itawamba think the world of him. He was good for the team.

........................................................................................................................

## Herman Bell
*Teammate, Itawamba Community College*
I met Wayne in 1978 at Itawamba College. We played basketball together for two years. We are the best of friends. He deserves his inductions. I wish him congratulations and best wishes on the book. He is a great friend to be around. He is there when you need him. I hope he receives everything that he deserves (*He needs to learn how to play golf*).

## Harvey *Goose* Giddens
*1978 teammate, Itawamba College*
Wayne loves helping people out. He has impeccable character professionally and always tries to do what's right. His game was fundamentally sound. He was a smart player, a good rebounder, and a scorer; his basketball skills were wonderful. He gives kids pointers and opportunities; helps to get them off the street. With Wayne what you see is what you get. I believe he has a bright future and that he is just getting started. He is very active and he lives the Word. He is the complete package.

## Kelvin *Hen* Henderson
*Teammate, Itawamba College*
I met Wayne in the fall of 1979, and we hit it right off. There were four of us from out of town - three from Memphis. He is a good guy and one can't help but to gravitate toward him. We couldn't go home

on the weekend, so Wayne would work on his game. I thought he was a square. He had a great work ethic. He kept jumping rope and running bleachers. He wanted to get better and hanging with him made us want to get better. He was such a happy-go-lucky guy. The Hall of Fame inductions are no surprise; he was the complete player. Wayne got more joy making a pass than scoring - very unselfish player. He was well liked; got it from his parents. He was very hospitable and was always helping someone else. We played one year at Itawamba together. He was ultra competitive and a real people person. We are still friends and keep in contact. He helped my son get a scholarship to a junior college.

**Ken Fortenberry**
*Coach, Southeastern Louisiana University*
I have nothing but good things to say about Wayne; he is one of a kind. If there were more people in the world like him, we would have a better world. My wife and I agree that he had great parents, who formed good traits early in life (for the entire family). He displayed great basketball skills - especially his outside-range shooting skills. I believe he could have made the pros. He was an unselfish player. We still keep in contact. He appreciates the opportunities he's been afforded. He is like a son to me.

## Don Wilson
*Assistant coach, Southeastern Louisiana University*
I worked with him two years; everybody loved him. Wayne was very unselfish, hardworking and goal oriented. He could play any position; it was like having another coach on the floor. Wayne is a positive person, who you can't say anything negative about. I've never seen him mad. He is a wonderful guy. He is aggressive and gets the job done. Wayne was one of the NCAA hosts. He was honest with the recruits; he laid it on the line. I think of Wayne often. His great attitude reflects his parents' upbringing. I'm proud to say that my son has some of Wayne's characteristics. We need more people in America like him. He is an ambassador to mankind.

## Larry Woolfolk
*1980 graduate assistant at SLU*
Wayne was always a man of impeccable character from start to finish, the epitome of an athlete. He was not arrogant or a hell raiser. He loved the game, but was all about getting his degree. He is like my little brother and always stays in touch. If I had one, I would want my son to pattern himself after Wayne. He is a real people person, a class act, a man ahead of his time.

## Tim Bowers
*Kingsbury teammate, SLU roommate*
We were childhood friends from the same neighborhood and teammates. We had strong family values, moral codes and attended church.

Our families were blue collar workers, who believed you should be part of the solution and not the problem. Playing basketball set the process for our career and working with kids. Wayne played recreational basketball for my father. He was a really good player and an even better person. He does good things in the city. Wayne believes in family and friends. He is basically a solid guy and a great humanitarian.

**Jerry Kelly**
*Teammate, Southeastern Louisiana University*
I met Wayne as a freshman during the 81-82 school year in Hammond, LA. We hit it off right away. Wayne was a leader and an all-around outstanding person. He was very accomplished. He had set goals, stayed focus, pursued and achieved his goals. Although he was on a basketball scholarship, education was number one. He was a leading scorer in 80-81, leading rebounder and MVP. He was selected all-independent his junior year and MVP during his senior year. He could play any position. It was amazing that at 6'6 he passed like a guard. He was a very unselfish player and carried everyone else on the team. I think his accolades are well deserved. No one gave him anything. I wish him well. He is a coach's dream.

......................................................................................................................................................................

## Larry Hymel
*SLU sports information director*

Wayne is the nicest kid we ever had. He was a gentleman, well dressed, polite, and very impressive. He was an excellent ball player - a team player, who carried himself well on the court just like off the court. He always responds to invitations to homecoming. I respect him. I am glad he was chosen for the Hall of Fame. He was a person that any athletic program would want to have.

## Gayle Neal
*President of SLU Alumni Association*

I became acquainted with Wayne Booker when he played basketball with Southeastern. I had coached for fifteen years and was the graduate assistant for the Southeastern basketball team the first year that Wayne's basketball coach, Ken Fortenberry, was head coach. Since Coach Fortenberry and I were close friends, we used to discuss Wayne and the type of player he was and his playing abilities. I could sense the admiration Coach Fortenberry had for Wayne as a person and as a player. Through that association I came to know Wayne and appreciate the person that he was and continues to be today. Each year we have a Southeastern basketball reunion and I get to visit with Wayne and keep up with him. On occasion he would come back for a game. Wayne always has conducted himself in a professional manner. He seems to always remember his alma mater by making himself available to help Southeastern recruit players; he has been especially helpful in the Memphis area in identifying potential college players.  When I served on the Southeastern Alumni Board, I was on the nominating committee to identify potential alumni board members.  Wayne was the first person that I thought of that would make a perfect board member and was happy to nominate him to the board.  His continued allegiance to Southeastern and his contribution to the alumni board have been remarkable.  It has certainly been a pleasure to see Wayne continue to grow to be a success, not only in his professional life, but his personal life as well.  I am thankful that we have had the opportunity to work together on the board and get to know Wayne even more and appreciate his abilities and support.  Southeastern is very fortunate to have graduates such as Wayne Booker and have him represent the alumni on the alumni board and in the professional field.

**Kathy Pittman**
*Director of SLU Alumni Association*
I have known Wayne Booker for about ten years and gotten to know him better each year as he attends both our annual reunion and the Hall of Fame events.  It was obvious that the respect he received from the administration and his colleagues went beyond his astounding sports ability and went to that of his character and accomplishments.  For this reason, he was nominated and recently elected to the

Alumni Association Board of Directors. He takes this responsibility, as he does all of his obligations, very seriously and does not miss a meeting, even though he has to come at his own expense from Memphis to Louisiana. We are pleased to have Wayne Booker as one of Southeastern's alumni.

### Melvin Lee
*Pastor, Macedonia Baptist Church Hyde Park*
Wayne is a man's man. He is a man of integrity, carries himself appropriately, and is a man of his word. I have known him for over twenty years. We met at Macedonia Baptist Church. He is ever mindful of people, who need his help and makes himself available. He shares the wisdom GOD has given him with young males and females. He is mindful of people, who GOD has placed in his life. He is personable on the court and aware of his athletic abilities. I watched him sharing tips on how to apply athletic skills to life. He has a knack for working with youth. He takes them on field trips and camping trips to teach them their roles as males. He is humble, which is a good quality not always seen in every man. Wayne doesn't look for accolades, but he is looking to make a difference. He is a family man, who exemplifies what the Word of GOD says of being the head of the family.

### Keith Norman
*Pastor, First Baptist Church Broad*
Congratulations on two Halls of Fame! It's a natural progression of GOD's purpose in Wayne's life. It's a powerful way through faith. Wayne uses his personal experiences to show GOD's grace through basketball, sports, and life experiences. Wayne believes in helping make someone better through opportunities. He is selfless and people call to inform him of others needing help. He is a bridge builder. Wayne is a friend, a great and outstanding person (*He is also the only Dallas Cowboys fan left.*). Our families travel together and it is an honor to know him. He lets others talk about his accolades, not himself. He is never boastful. He wants to help the youth; he wants them to be productive citizens. I think his induction into the Halls of Fame from where he started is a great accomplishment. It's like living a dream. It's a testament to hard work, dedication, belief, and commitment rolled into one. That equals success. He's good people.

### Penny Hardaway
*Former NBA player*
I watched Wayne play basketball at the Hollywood Community Center. He was a strong force and the best in the neighborhood. I always wanted to compete against the best, so I wanted to compete against Wayne. Wayne could jump up, hit the ball on the front of the rim intentionally and then dunk it. I admired him from childhood.

## Elliott Perry
*Former NBA player*
I have known Wayne since the 9th or 10th grade. We met through Michael Toney at the Hollywood Community Center. Wayne has been a good mentor. He is a good guy to be around on and off the court. I looked up to him and respected him. He is well deserving of his inductions. He is accomplished on the court and off. He consistently has a wonderful attitude and is very helpful.

## Andre Turner
*Former NBA player*
I met Wayne in high school. We competed in the Bluff City Classic. He was a student of basketball. He would study the player and the personality of the player. He was the hardest worker – rebounding and assisting, although not the tallest. He only played one year of high school basketball and excelled to get better because of earlier rejection. He took total advantage of an opportunity and ran with it. He's extra giving, laid back, and quiet. I believe Wayne has a lot to share. People are blessed by him. I wish him the best.

## Jim Dandy
*Rock singer*
I know Wayne through his brother, Ronald, and I have never met a Booker that I didn't like. Although Wayne was a late bloomer because he didn't play basketball until his senior year in high school, he

is the top of the line.  He is definitely top shelf.  Wayne is a straight ahead, man of his word, all-round good guy.  You can't help but feel good when you are around him.  I think his getting inducted twice is a great thing; Wayne is worthy of it.  He is a great ball player and a very humble person.  He is a winner - perfect example of the old adage that winners never quit and quitters never win.

**Ned Booker Sr.**
*Father*
I went to the gym and played basketball with my sons.  When Wayne was coming up in high school, I didn't really think about his going on to college and being so successful.  I am happy that he made it, and I wish him much success with the book.

**Narvel Louise Booker-Ware**
*Sister*
Wayne has displayed excellent characteristics from childhood to adulthood.  He is an exceptional role model for the younger generation in both our family and the community.  He is well respected and known in the Hyde Park and Kingsbury community.  Our mom would be so proud of him.  I believe she is looking down on him happily, and her spirit is here with him and us.  It is because of our parents' training that Wayne is the person that he is.  It is a wonderful accomplishment to make two Halls of Fame, and it is well deserved.  The committee made a superb decision when they chose him on both occasions.  I wish him the best with his book and in his endeavors.

### Robert Booker
*Brother*

Wayne worked hard all his life - going to college, playing ball and accomplished his goals. I think it's wonderful. I thought he would achieve his goal because he has a love for basketball. I am glad he was inducted into the two Halls of Fame. I am happy he had the opportunity to try out with the pros.

### Ned Booker Jr.
*Brother*

It is a great privilege to see baby brother receive the awards. He accomplished something that is very rare and is the first one in the family to receive. He started late, but gave it his all. I believe growing up as a family taught him some things. Mom and Dad contributed to his being who he is.

### Larry Booker
*Brother*

All supported him, but had a little doubt in sports because he was soft. His senior in high school he got tough. We played together through his senior year. Our parents' upbringing had a lot to do with his character on the floor. He helped kids and other coaches. Kids are the joy of his heart. He is willing to help anyone. He got basketball traits from our dad.

## Ronald Booker
*Brother*

I am happy to see what he went through got him where he is with honors. Fun and play turned into competitive nature. Achievement wasn't a goal. Classic to receive Hall of Fame, not once, but twice! I have heartfelt excitement for my brother. It's like fireworks on New Year's Eve and the 4th of July combined. Wayne didn't talk about Hall of Fame, which makes it great. The road travelled to get there is what touches him. I am beyond proud of my brother. Hall of Fame is icing on the cake.

## Kim McManis
*Cousin*

Wayne and I played ball together on the recreational side. His being inducted into two Halls of Fame is a great accomplishment and well deserved. Wayne is an exceptional athlete. He ran track, but he is a much better basketball player. He is a role model for a lot of kids. Wayne is very popular. If they had cell phones in outer space, ET wouldn't phone home; he would phone Wayne. I wish him much success and hope GOD continues to bless him in all his endeavors.

## Terry Johnson
*Cousin*

I think it is incredible that he earned inductions into the Hall of Fame from both schools that he attended. A player very seldom makes it once, but twice is a great accomplishment. Wayne is a class act. He comes from a basketball family. I moved to Memphis from St. Louis because of Wayne's help. There is a Scripture in the Bible that says faith without works is dead. Wayne is very inspirational because he continually lives by his faith and works. He is a very popular, helpful and giving person. He helps without worrying about it or thinking about it. People should pattern themselves after him. I think that someone should give their kid this book as a motivation. It shows where he came from compared to where is he now. The kid will know it can happen for them, too.

## Willie Kimmons, Ph.D
*Cousin*

I think it is an outstanding achievement for Wayne to get inducted into both Halls of Fame. This is one of the highest honors an individual can accomplish in a lifetime. I'm very proud and delighted to be associated with Mr. Wayne Booker. He is an outstanding role model for the younger generation. GOD bless and GOD keep him. Mr. Wayne Booker's character is beyond reproach. He is a risk taker and a high achiever. He is utilizing his GOD-given talent to further his personal and professional goals to help others. Wayne Booker is morally sound and extremely focused on accomplishing his mission.

### Joseph Norman Sr.
*Community coach, park commission team*
I was coaching two teams and decided to coach three. Wayne was on my senior team. I met him through my son. I had a talk with him and saw Wayne play pickup games. I asked if he wanted to play for me. Wayne had heard of my reputation, so he decided to play for me. He would do whatever was asked of him. He was a versatile player, who played forward and center. He started all of the games. He was very interested in all of basketball. He was exceptional on basketball IQs. A lot of coaches began to watch him; Kingsbury coaches wanted him. He became the top basketball player. He blossomed into such a good player in high school, college coaches started to recruit him with offer letters. He would come by to visit when he was in town. He was an all-around person, who learned basketball well and was good academically. He is humble, articulate and kind. He is deserving of all accolades. Wayne gives youth the direction they need to achieve the highest grade of success. I highly respect Wayne and his family. He is an outstanding person in basketball and life.

## Gary S Greer
*Friend, former coach*
I learned to shine shoes at Bland's Barber Shop, where Wayne and his older brothers shined shoes. I have known Wayne from the 'hood for over 30 years. I see the Hand of God as it continues to manifest in his life, and thus he has been blessed with the two-time achievement from both his alma maters. He is a man of great faith, integrity and character. It is an honor to know him. He also happens to be a member of the greatest fraternity the world has ever known – Omega Psi Phi, Inc. Yes, he's my fraternity brother [I guess you could tell.]. I also had the opportunity to coach Wayne on one of our company teams. The team was comprised of former college and semi-pro players, ex-overseas and former high school standouts. We participated in grueling double elimination tournaments of 9 to 13 games over a two-day period. We were the undisputed champs for several years, winning in Dallas several times, Atlanta, Houston, and Memphis, as well. Everyone hated to see the Memphis Bad Boys coming and Wayne was leading the charge running the point and posting up at will.

## John Dunavant
*Operations VP, Memphis-based Fortune 500 Company*
I met Wayne at work after hearing that he was active in helping young high school kids in the Memphis area get introduced for consideration to various college programs. After meeting him, I then remembered

about his successes in being from Memphis and in playing basketball at SLU. Wayne has been successful at basketball everywhere he has played, from Kingsbury High to Itawamba CC to SLU. The fact that he is in the Hall of Fame of both of his college alma maters speaks for itself. He is one of the best of the best to have played at both institutions. More impactful than his basketball skills is Wayne the person. He has helped a number of young kids in this area continue to play basketball, but more importantly, to continue on with their education. Unfortunately, college recruiting, i.e., the AAU circuit, has really left many parents and young kids with a bad perception and perhaps a reality of the recruiting process. Wayne has helped manage through the issues with many kids and parents and has given advice and pointed them in the right direction. At the end of the day, it is never about him, it's about who he is helping. I consider him a great mentor and friend.

**Pat Carter**
*Businessman and former church member*
I have known Wayne since he was a young man. I attended church with his family. I knew he would do a lot of justice to himself and his family. He enables and inspires his family to do well. I am very glad for his inductions. Wayne is driving a good road. I believe his book is good for the family and community.

**Darryl Braden**

*Childhood friend*

We grew up in the same neighborhood. Our mothers were friends and co-workers. We have known each other all of our lives. Wayne is an outstanding individual. He has great family values, is GOD fearing, and is a special person. He is an exemplary athlete all the time. His peers recognize that he is special. He is going to every top selected group. Getting inducted twice speaks for itself.

**Jerald Stark**
*Childhood friend*

We grew up in the same neighborhood two blocks apart. We played basketball in the recreational league and on the playground. He is an outstanding player. His accomplishments are well deserved. Wayne represents his family, community, and himself as well. I am very proud of him. Congratulations, and it's amazing to see where he comes from and compare it to where he is going.

**Larry Thomas**
*Childhood friend*

Wayne and I have been friends for over 30 years and have maintained a very good relationship. We are from the same neighborhood, where we grew up together. Our families know each other very well. It really does not surprise me to hear that Wayne has been inducted into two Halls of Fame. He has always demonstrated a strong will to excel and to be the best at what he does. Wayne has always been the epitome of a team player. His character is unquestionable. Everyone that has ever come into contact with him has always had kind words to say about Wayne. I can truly say that Wayne has always been trustworthy and a man of his word.

## Dwight Boyd
*Friend*
Twenty years ago Wayne and I met while playing pick-up basketball in the summer league. His inductions speak volumes about how hard he works in the classroom and on the court. I think the definition of character is the way a person carries himself in public. Wayne does a great job with that and also in the community with the youth.

## Curtis Green
*Friend*
I met Wayne twenty-five years ago, when I saw him playing ball at the community center. We competed against each other. He was the gentle giant - tough on the floor, but a good guy. I am real proud that he made his accomplishments; a lot of guys don't. We also played in developmental league. He was real competition and a joy to be around.

## Anthony Hilliard

*Friend*

I met Wayne as a competitor on the basketball court playing in a 3-on-3 championship tournament in Downtown Memphis. While playing against him, I thought he was very good and thought of having Wayne on the same team. We played on several teams after our initial meeting. He is a good person, has a good heart, and is a man of his word. He is helpful and genuine. I think they couldn't have inducted a better person. It's an excellent accomplishment to get inducted twice after only playing one year of high school ball. He is a great gentle person. He is the same every time you see him.

## Howard Richardson

*Friend*

I know Wayne as a friend and a competitor. We met at a basketball summer league at Cypress Jr. High School. He always thinks of others before himself. I always say character is what you are when people are not looking. Wayne Booker has impeccable character. He comes from a GOD-fearing family and was raised with that old fashioned Christian upbringing that has somehow, for the most part, been lost in today's society. If you ever had Sunday dinner at his home, when all his family was living, you would know exactly what I mean. To be inducted into any Hall of Fame is an unbelievable accomplishment, but to be inducted into two (Halls of Fame) is a lifetime achievement.

Wayne is a special person and fantastic things are reserved for the type of person he is. I think Wayne's life story will inspire the kids of today to strive to meet any goal they have in life. I have and always will respect Wayne Booker.

**McKinley Singleton, Jr.**
*Friend, former NBA player*
Wayne and I met in '78 at a basketball tournament: Kingsbury vs. Booker T Washington. Wayne was guarding me. There couldn't be a better friend or man than Wayne Booker. He's a loyal person, who speaks his mind. He is someone you want to call friend. Getting inducted is an honor within itself, and to be chosen by one's colleagues is a great honor. Wayne is one of the best to come through the schools. He helped the school as well as the athletic program. His character is what got him inducted. I pray GOD continues to bless him to overcome. I wish him well in his future endeavors and may GOD continue to bless Wayne to achieve what he has for him.

**Larry Spicer**
*Friend*
I met Wayne during his college years. We played summer league in his later years. It was all about basketball. He was a very good player and person. He was easy to get along with. He was a class act.

Wayne is an example that dreams do come true. He gets respect from his peers, which is well deserved. He was a hard and dedicated worker and was determined to be the best.

## Clarence Swearengen
*Friend and mentee*
Wayne and I met in 1977 at Kingsbury High School. I think of Wayne as a big brother, mentor, and athlete. Our families lived in same area. I have a lot of respect for him and always looked up to him. I have modeled some of my ways from Wayne's teaching. He is one of the first black males coming from our neighborhood I've known to be inducted. I am very proud of him. I watched Wayne play his entire career. I could tell Wayne would do well in life. He has great values and work ethics. He exemplified those characteristics and stayed focused on his goals. He is connected with the right people and with CHRIST.

## Wamon Buggs
**Former USFL & NFL player, line fraternity brother**
Wayne and I met as basketball competitors. He was a good player and a great coach. We pledged Omega Psi Phi together in 1989. He is GOD fearing and works well with kids. He is very deserving of his honors and earned his inductions. We need more like him. I am proud of him for making Hall of Fame twice.

## James Harvey Jr.
*Team player, mentee*

I met Wayne in 1998, when he was my middle school basketball coach at Lausanne Collegiate School. I played for him one year and have been with him ever since. He is a father figure for me. Wayne Booker really cares about kids and their futures. He is not as concerned about the athletic aspect as much as he is concerned with developing young men and women to become productive citizens. There is no one better deserving as far as touching people's lives - especially young men. I think his two-time Hall of Fame inductions are well deserved.

## Amorrow Morgan
*Basketball player, mentee*

I met Wayne through my father, when both of them were members of First Baptist Church Broad. When I was a junior in high school, Wayne said if my grades were good he could help me with scholarships; he was a man of his word. He is a good guy, who is extremely skilled and intelligent. He is a legend for helping kids – male and female. I was impressed that he was inducted, not only into one, but two Halls of Fame. It makes sense that they would induct him because of his skills and intelligence. He really deserves the inductions. I admire him in every aspect of his life. He is a strong Christian man and has inspired me to be a better man. He goes out of his way to help people; strangers he encounters, who need his help, are included. He doesn't do it for a payment of any kind; he does it because he has a good heart. He took me under his wing when my father died. He is now a father figure for me. He keeps in touch and checks on me. Wayne Booker networks well. He is a good guy, great family man, and just a good person all around. He is a great people person and will help many more. He deserves anything good that comes to him in the near future. And I believe something good is in the works for him.

# SPEECHES

### Itawamba Community College

Good afternoon. I'd like to thank GOD for receiving this honor to-day. I'd also like to thank Itawamba Community College Alumni Association for selecting me to the Hall of Fame. I'd like to say thanks to Coach Nute for giving me a chance to play high school basketball. He was the only coach, who gave me a chance. I had tried out for so many times that I lost confidence. So I would like to thank him as well. Coach Nute gave Wiley Jefferson, one of my team mates, and I a ride to Itawamba in 1978. And Wiley Jefferson picked Jackson State Community College in Jackson, TN. I told Wiley I've got to sign with Itawamba Community College and I have never regretted it from that day on. I'd like to recognize some of my ex-teammates from high school, who helped pave the way...Tim Bowers, the late Jerome Deener, John Harper, Will Thomas, the late Bruce Whitmore, Bobby Broyles, Donnie Cox and Clarence Hawkins. I thank them as well for supporting me. I'd also like to thank Coach Newsome who is not here today due to a death in the family. I'd like to thank Coach Newsome and Itawamba Community College for giving me a scholar-ship. I really thank them. I'd like to say a special thanks to Coach Newsome because this is where my education career started, as well as my basketball career. Coach Newsome was more than a coach. He always gave me good advice on and off the court and never had a problem. People wondered how I made the decision of what school I was going to go to after I left Itawamba Community College. It was kind of easy because Coach Newsome played at Southeastern, and that's where I ended up signing as well. So that was an easy choice because I wanted to follow in his footsteps. To my teammates, Shelton Thomas, Herman Bell, Harvey Goose Giddens, Kelvin Hen Henderson, Marty Too-Too Coleman, Demac Coleman, and Randy Hilliard, thanks, you guys. Shelton, thanks for getting open so I could make an assist. Herman, thanks for the alley-oops, so I could dunk and the crowds would cheer for us. Thanks to Harvey Goose Giddens, a freshman at the time, that helped me with my fundamentals. There were two brothers, Marty Too-Too Coleman and Willie DeMac Coleman from Baldwyn, Mississippi. They really pushed me in practice every day and Randy Hillard, who took me under his wing when I was a freshman. He showed me the ropes and Kevin Moore along with Ray Hudson for being great teammates. I would like to thank my family for supporting me while I attended ICC. I know my family notices how differently Hwy 78 looks because we traveled some weaving roads. I would like to thank my dad Ned Booker, my mother Bobbie Jean Booker, who has gone on to be with the LORD. I can just see her smiling down on me because we made so many trips here. I would like to thank my sister, Narvel Louise, thanks for packing so many boxes for us and taking care of me and out-of-state players. I was telling some friends how they used to give us $10.00 a weekend and we had to make it stretch from Friday through Sunday. Thanks, Louise. I would like to thank my brothers, Robert, Ned Jr., Larry (Bull) and Ron, for supporting me while at ICC. I would like to thank my family, friends and church members. I had some great times at ICC and Coach and I speak with each other often. I will never forget ICC and if there's anything you need, feel free to call me. Lastly, I would like to give a special thanks to ICC for inducting me into the Athletic Hall of Fame.


## Southeastern Louisiana University

Good evening. First I'd like to thank GOD for this day. I'd like to thank Southeastern for selecting me to be in the Hall of Fame with the other two inductees. I just want to tell a quick story right quick. Most people don't know that I only played one year of high school ball. I'd like to thank Coach Nute for giving me the chance because I had tried out so many years. No one would give me a chance. I played 7th and 8th grade ball, but that was it. After that I got to Kingsbury High School, this coach, Coach Nute, stand up again. He gave me a chance and also I had some coaches I want to recognize and call their names to give them recognition: Coach Phillips - YMCA, Coach Odell Harris - 7th grade, Joseph Norman, Sr. - community center ball, Coach Brogan - Cypress Junior High, 8th grade and one year of high school. Coach Wayne Newsome at Itawamba gave me a chance and that is how I ended up at SLU. But when I came to SLU, Coach Fortenberry gave me that chance and I remember these words like it was yesterday. He said, "Wayne, if you bust your butt in the classroom, you may not make the pros, but you'll get your degree and have something to fall back on." There was a coach here, Larry Woolfolk. Please stand. Wave your hand. He was the grad assistant when I was here. I can remember his words like yesterday. He used to make us run up and down the steps on the bleachers on the back side of Southeastern past Strawberry Stadium, and these were his exact same words, "It's hard, but it's fair. If you had a good home you chose to come to SLU, so make the best of it." I'd like to give recognition to Don Wilson, a former player and Hall of Famer who would tell me, "Wayne, bust your butt!" I tried to do that every day at practice and in the classroom. I'd like to thank my teammates as well. And lastly, I would to thank Coach Fortenberry, who is not here, but I talk to him all the time. That man would always push us. Regardless of what he would make you go to class and play ball. If you're down ten he'd make you think you were up ten. But I'd like to thank Coach Newsome again and Coach Fortenberry and Coach Nute for allowing me to have the chance to play ball and get my degree and my selections to the Hall of Fame. Thanks to SLU and my family as well. Thank you.

# Southeastern Athletics Hall of Fame

**Wayne Booker**
*Induction Class of 2008*
*Men's Basketball*

Wayne Booker played two seasons for the Lions as they were making the transition to Division I status and playing as an independent in the NCAA. He was a two-time All-Southeastern Independent selection and was an all-Louisiana pick in 1981-82.

He led the Lions in scoring once and twice led the team in assists. He still ranks among the all-time rebound leaders and helped Southeastern two winnings seasons in its first two years in Division I competition. He was inducted into the Itawamba Community College Hall of Fame in 2005.